MARRIAGE
By God's Design

MARRIAGE
By God's Design

"Discover some of the most powerful revelation on the mystery of Oneness as it is contained in God's original design for marriage..."

"...they are no more two, but one flesh."
   Genesis:2:24; Mark:10:8; Ephesians:5:31

C. BERNARD MCBRIDE
PASTOR & TEACHER

Marriage, By God's Design

by Pastor & Teacher, C. Bernard McBride

Copyright © 2017, C. Bernard McBride

Cover Designed by EB-Printing

All rights reserved. This book is protected under the copyright laws of the United States of America. No portion of this publication may be reproduced, stored in electronic systems or transmitted in any form or by any means, electronic, recording, mechanical, photocopy or otherwise, without prior permission from C. Bernard McBride. The use of brief quotations for personal or group study, or literary reviews are permitted. All Scriptures quoted in this book are from the King James Version of the Bible unless otherwise noted.

Published by: C. Bernard McBride

9203 Highway 6 S, Ste#124-134

Houston Texas 77083

ISBN: 978-0-692-82893-9

For Worldwide Distribution

Printed in the United States of America

First Printing: 2017

Dedication

I dedicate this book to my beautiful wife, friend and life-long companion, Pastor Nicolle McBride! I so honor, value and appreciate her as one of God's greatest gifts to me! Together, we share in the celebration of twenty-seven years of marriage; four wonderful kids, and fourteen beautiful grandchildren! She was extremely instrumental in introducing me to Christ, and became a major tool in the hand of God to help cultivate me into the man of God I am today!

Baby, we have weathered many storms, faced many challenges and endured many hardships – but you have remained constant through it all! You have proved yourself to be my "ride or die" in this life! You are truly a Proverbs thirty-one Woman; a virtuous woman! *"Your price is indeed far above rubies, and my heart does safely trust in you!"* Sweetheart, I love you! And thank you for taking life's journey with me!

Acknowledgments

First and foremost, I give all praise and glory to our great God and Savior, Jesus Christ, from Whom all Blessings flow! Blessed be His Name forevermore, Amen… It is because of Him that we live, move and have our very existence (Acts:17:28) – and without Him, we are nothing!

When I take into consideration all of the struggles that my wife and I endured during the first several years of our marriage, I would have never thought in my wildest imagination that God would raise me up to write a book on marriage! But it was through all of the highs and lows, ups and downs, joys and pains of life that God used as a means to give me access and insight into some of His greatest mysteries involving His love and character! Truly, I am grateful and humbled that He would even consider me for the assignment of penning what I've learned in a book to be a blessing to others!

To my Mom, the late Dora E. McBride – a precious jewel; a rare-find, and a tremendous gift to all her children! She too was a woman of virtue – the Bible says that *"her children shall rise up, and call her blessed"* (*Prov:31:28*)! During her time upon this earth, she was that voice of reasoning for me, and a tremendous source of strength and encouragement! I personally witnessed her struggle as a single-parent, how that she sacrificed so much just to provide for, and support her family. She became my "SHERO!" And one of my primary goals in life was to see her happy, and to make her proud!

"So in loving memory Mom – this book is a testament of your labor and legacy that you left behind in me!"

To my spiritual father and mother – the late Dr. Stanley Diggs and his beautiful wife, Elder Denise Diggs of Love Divine Family Worship Center of Baltimore, Maryland, who hath begotten me in the faith – bringing me into the saving knowledge of our Lord Jesus Christ and nurtured me in the Kingdom! Words cannot express the love and appreciation that I have towards you, and the many years of dedication that you've given to the service of God... You gave to me the gift that keeps on giving – the gift of Jesus Christ! And it is my chief aim to prove that your work (in me) was not in vain!

To *"the treasured gifts"* that now shepherd us in ministry – Apostle Jerome Nelson Sr. (a.k.a. Dad), and Pastor Betty Nelson (a.k.a. Mom) of Spirit of Life Ministries, Houston, Texas: "Oh, how precious you are!" You were there for us during some of the toughest times in our lives – the passing of our dear Bishop, Dr. Diggs, and the passing of my beloved mom who went Home to be with the Lord just a few months apart from each other. No doubt, God foresaw that the turbulent times were coming, and He strategically placed you in our lives to help get us through the pain! You have loved and supported us from that time, and have not ceased! And we are so grateful to have you in our lives, as you aid in overseeing the work that God has entrusted to us!

And last, but certainly not least – to the greatest Church on planet earth ☺, Soldiers for Christ World Ministries, Inc. of Houston, Texas – where I am the proud Pastor of some of the most beautiful, tenacious, resilient, loving, Spirit-filled believers! Soldiers for Christ, you bring me so much joy and fulfillment! For it was "in Christ" that I had begotten you through the gospel. Your love, support and unwavering commitment to the Gospel and dedication to ministry is noteworthy – and I am so honored to serve as your leader! I want you to always know that you hold a very special place in my heart – you always will…

Table of Contents

Dedication

Acknowledgments

INTRODUCTION 1

CHAPTER 1
Sex Outside of Marriage 7
    Fornication 10
    Adultery 11
    Shacking-Up 14

CHAPTER 2
The Sanctity of Marriage 17

CHAPTER 3
The Structure of Marriage 21

CHAPTER 4
The Purpose of Marriage 29
    The Reality of God's Love 30
    The Key Characteristics of Agapē 32
    Agapē Reveals Character 35

CHAPTER 5
The Mystery of Oneness 37

CHAPTER 6
Singleness to Oneness 49
    Singleness 49

Single, but Celibate 53

Marriage is a Choice 55

The Process of Becoming One 59

CHAPTER 7

Vision for Marriage 63

CHAPTER 8

Roles & Responsibilities in Marriage 73

The Role and Responsibilities of the Husband 75

The Role and Responsibilities of the Wife 81

CHAPTER 9

Understanding the One I Love 87

Pessimism 89

Optimism 89

Introverts 91

Extroverts 92

Assuming Good-will 93

CHAPTER 10

The Bedroom of the Believer 95

CHAPTER 11

Is Divorce a Biblical Option? 103

The Most Common Reasons for Divorce 107

Separation 109

The Importance of Premarital Counseling 110

Abuse in Marriage 111

Is Divorce Forgivable? 112

CHAPTER 12

A Guide to Premarital Counseling......................... 115

Suggested Topics for Discussion 116

INTRODUCTION

Marriages are the bedrock of every family! They are the foundation upon which stable families are built. However, with each passing generation, we see society's view on marriage constantly changing, and veering further and further away from God's original design!

Being that marriage was the very first institution ever established by God between two people, one might think that as a society, we'd be experts on the subject by now. Instead, over 6,000 marriages are conducted daily in the United States, and nearly fifty percent of them end in divorce, both inside and outside the church. So it would appear that we're still fumbling around in the dark on this matter.

As we know it, the world today is trying to redefine marriage by instituting laws that are clearly against God's Will. Some suggest that the Biblical view of marriage is old and outdated; that times have changed, and that it's view is even radical or extreme. But what they fail to realize is that, (1) God's Word is not open for debate, and (2) He never changes, and neither does His Word:

Mt:24:35

*Jesus said, Heaven and earth shall pass away, but **my words shall not pass away**.*

1Pt:1:23

*Peter said, Being born again, not of corruptible seed, but of **incorruptible**, by **the word of God**, which **liveth** and **abideth for ever**.*

The Lord commanded Ezekiel to eat *"the whole roll,"* meaning to eat ALL of His Word (*Ez:3:1-4*). And that's one of the world's biggest problems, and even some believers – they don't want to eat *the whole roll*. The truth is, either we believe God's Word, or we don't! As committed Believers, we don't have the luxury of picking and choosing what we want to adhere to in God's Word. If we're His children, and we believe that His Word is true, then we must eat the whole roll and realize that His Word is eternal and it has not, it does not, nor will it EVER change!

If a person truly love and reverence God in their life, no matter how society changes, it could never get them to go against God's Word! Because they understand that when it's all said and done, you still have to give an account to God for the things you do and allow. Jesus said, "If a man love me, *he will* keep my words (John:14:23)". Therefore our love and reverence for God is demonstrated through our obedience! Undoubtedly, there *will be times* when Christians will have to take *a stand* for their faith and obey God when society create scenarios that oppose His Word.

> 2Timothy:4:3-4
>
> *For the time will come when they will not endure sound doctrine; but after their own lusts shall they heap to themselves teachers, having itching ears; And they shall*

turn away their ears from the truth, and shall be turned unto fables.

When the apostles were thrown in prison for preaching in the name of Jesus, God sent an angel to set them free! The angel of the Lord commanded them to *go, stand* and *preach all the Words* of this life. When the officials found them in the temple teaching again in Jesus' Name, the high priest had them brought before the council and asked them, *"Did we not command you to cease from preaching in His (Jesus) name?"* The apostles replied, *"We ought to obey God rather than men (Acts:5:29)."* This should be the position of every Bible believing Christian whenever law or society contradicts God's Word.

So, we must get back on track in our marriages and family! There is only One Source to turn to for answers and a clear understanding on the *sanctity, structure* and *purpose* of marriage, as well as, how to achieve *"absolute oneness"* in this incredible Covenant – and that Source is God!

Always bear this in mind, *"man cannot alter what he did not author."* Therefore, no matter how society tries to ignore, omit, discredit or disregard the Word of God, attempting to exclude God from their way of life, He cannot be dismissed! They will still have to answer to Him in the end! Societies may change, their governments and laws may change – but God and His Word never changes.

Chapter 1

Sex Outside of Marriage

Sex is one of the most beautiful, intimate and sacred expressions of love that God has given to committed Covenant relationships. It is a gift intended to be a blessing to marriages, but has became widely misused, abused and perverted by mankind over the centuries to satisfy their own fleshly lusts.

God purposed sex to be 'the seal of commitment' between a man and woman in Covenant. He never intended sex to be used in any other relationship that wasn't defined by the Covenant of marriage. In the event that sex did occur outside of, or prior to marriage under the law, God would still expect them to solidify their relationship by marriage – otherwise the act would become sin to those individuals:

Ex:22:16

And if a man entice a maid that is not betrothed, and lie with her, he shall surely endow her to be his wife. KJV

By no means am I endorsing, condoning or encouraging sex before marriage by bringing up this point. I'm merely highlighting the fact that it was never intended to be used in any other relationship besides marriage. And that God took such a serious issue with it, that He expected them to marry should sex occur under those circumstances.

The Scripture demanded that they marry! Of course, some will dispute and say, "but that was under the law, and we're not under the law, but under grace!" And that's so True, but only in the sense that we're not saved, nor justified (or declared righteous) by "the works of the law", but we're saved and justified (or declared righteous) by "grace through faith" that we may obey in the newness of the spirit

(Rom:7: 6; Gal:2:16; Eph:2:8-10). What am I saying, "Now that we are saved (rescued from the penalty of eternal death), we obey!" Remember, Jesus did not come to destroy the law or the prophets, but He came to fulfill; or fully live-out every Word through obedience – so that we who believe could be justified through His righteousness (Mt:5:17; Rom:5:19; Rom:8:3-4)!

Exodus:22:16 reveals God's intent for the type of relationship in which sex was to be used. Then Paul solidifies this *line of thought* by warning that a man should marry to avoid the sin of *fornication*!

> 1Cor:7:2:
>
> *Nevertheless, **to avoid** fornication, let **every man** have his own wife, and let **every woman** have her own husband. KJV*

The only way a person can *"avoid; prevent; or stay out of the way of"* the sin of fornication is by every man having his *"own wife"* and every woman having her *"own husband"*!

Giving reverence and obedience to this principle keeps the believer in a *"right (non-offensive) relationship with God."*

Fornication

Merriam-Webster Dictionary defines *fornication* as the consensual sexual relationship between two persons who are *not married* to each other; sex outside the covenant of marriage. However, most Bible Dictionaries inarguably define it as *"sexual immorality"*. So, considering its Biblical definition, we better understand that having sex with a person whom you have no intentions of marrying, or that you do not follow-thru with your intentions of marriage, means that you've cross the boundaries set by God and have entered into *"sexual immorality"* (which falls into a category such as sexual perversion, abuse or misuse).

Fornication in the Greek is *porneía* (it's the root of the English words "pornography, pornographic"), which is derived from *pernaō*, and means "to sell off" – in a proper rendering, it means *"a selling off* (or surrendering) *of sexual purity"*. Covering any and every type of *promiscuity*.

God is fully aware of all our sexual desires, after all, He created them within the body. However, these passions can get out of control when they are exposed to perversion, abuse or misuse. Nonetheless, His intentions for sex remains the same, it's His gift to you and your spouse within the confines of marriage. If you are able to exercise control over your fleshly desires as a Single, you do well! But if you cannot contain; if you are unable and have little-to-no restraint over your sexual desires, then the Scripture strongly suggests that you marry in order to have those needs met, and that you maintain a right relationship with God. Those who have absolutely no intentions of marrying should completely abstain from sexual intimacy and seek God for self-control – otherwise it will lead to trouble in the flesh and sin before God.

Adultery

Merriam-Webster Dictionary defines *adultery* as the consensual sexual relationship with someone other than your legal spouse. In other words, one *who is married*, but consents to a sexual relationship with someone else to whom they are *not married*. This definition agrees with the Biblical meaning of the word, but the Bible takes it a step further by revealing how seriously God views this act – not only does He see it as *evil*, but under the law, it was an act that *warranted death*.

> *Deut:22:22*
>
> *If a man be found lying with a woman married to an husband, then they shall both of them die, both the man that lay with the woman, and the woman: so shalt thou put away evil from Israel. KJV*

One of the reasons that these sins are so serious is because – not only are you acting out of your own lustful desires, but they involve or influence others to participate in the sin (Rom:1:24-32).

God has absolutely *no problem with sex,* as long as it's within the legal confines of marriage! God honors the bedroom of the married, but He takes a major issue when sex is misused, abused or perverted! The writer in Hebrews says that *"those are the ones"* that God WILL JUDGE!

Heb:13:4

Marriage is honourable in all, and the bed undefiled: but whoremongers and adulterers God will judge. KJV

1Cor:6:9-11

*Know ye not that the unrighteous shall not inherit the kingdom of God? Be not deceived: **neither fornicators**, nor idolaters, nor **adulterers**, nor **effeminate** (male prostitutes, NLT), nor **abusers of themselves with mankind** (men who practice homosexuality, NLT), nor thieves, nor covetous, nor drunkards, nor revilers, nor extortioners, shall inherit the kingdom of God. And such were some of you: but ye are washed, but ye are sanctified, but ye are justified in the name of the Lord Jesus, and by the Spirit of our God. KJV*

So, if we've been redeemed by the blood of Jesus; if we are now the children of God, then *that's not us anymore!* But if we're still practicing those kinds of lifestyles, then obviously, we have not been washed and are still in our sin!

Shacking-Up

To *live with* or *shack-up with* someone, and exercise all the rights and privileges of a married couple without actually committing yourself in a legally binding Covenant agreement with them – is disobedience to God's Word. In such cases, God is in *no way obligated* to honor and recognize that union as a legitimate marriage! Consider what Jesus said to the woman at the well:

Jn:4:16-18

Jesus saith unto her, Go, call thy husband, and come hither. The woman answered and said, I have no husband. Jesus said unto her, **Thou hast well said, I have no husband***: For thou hast had* **five** *husbands; and* **he** *whom thou* **now hast** *is* **not thy husband***: in that saidst thou truly.*

As the human race, man is always trying to find a way to negate, omit or go around God's Word, and justify their actions because of their sinful/rebellious nature. But this ought not be so with the redeemed of God. We should be seeking and striving in every way to align our hearts in sincere obedience to God. And God is clear about His Will for both the Single and married lifestyles where sex is concerned. For those who have no desire to marry, or may not be ready for marriage – God expects them to honor Him by exercising control over their bodies, while rendering to Him dedicated service (*1Cor:7:32-35*). For those who are ready for marriage, or who feel sexually troubled in their flesh, God provides a way of escape through marriage – so that there be no distractions in your devotion to Him (*1Cor:7:2,9&36*). But anyone who chooses to continue in the willful practice and lifestyles of sexual sin, God will not hold them guiltless (*1Cor:6:18; 2Cor:5:10*).

Chapter 2

The Sanctity of Marriage

Marriage is a sacred Covenant! And what makes it so sacred is the Biblical fact that marriage IS NOT manmade – but marriage was designed by God! This means that He holds the exclusive rights to its entire make-up and constitution! For it was God Who instituted marriage in the Garden of Eden:

    Gen:2:18

> *...the LORD God said, "It is NOT GOOD that man should be alone; I will make a help-meet for him (or a helper; a companion; a suitable partner). KJV*

God uses the term *"alone"* to describe Adam's existence. "Alone," not *"lonely"*. The term "alone" is translated as "all-one" or "all-in-one". This helps us to understand that Adam was complete within himself, for he was a direct replica of God in the natural. But then, God put Adam to sleep and took "out of him" (*that is, out of his own flesh*) everything He needed to make him "*a wife*" for him (*Verse:21*).

It's important to note that God did not go back into the dust of the ground to create Woman. In fact, the Bible doesn't even use the term "create" to describe her formation, although she was indeed created. The Scripture says that He "made" the Woman (*Gen:2:22*) from Adam's rib. And the term "made" signifies that she was fashioned from the preexistence of Adam. God went inside of the Man which He had created, and took out *the necessary DNA* to make, or form "the perfect companion" for him. So actually, the

Woman was an *offspring* of Adam – "because she was *taken out of man (Gen:2:23)*".

> 1Cor:11:8-9
>
> "For the man is not of the woman, but the woman of the man. Neither was the Man created for the woman, but the woman for the man." KJV
>
> Verse:12:
>
> "For as the woman is "of the man", even so is the man also "by the woman", but all things of God." KJV

Which is to say, that although "the woman" is made from the man, man (or *lit.* mankind or humanity) is given birth "by the woman".

The Bible proves emphatically that marriage is not *by any means* a manmade institution, but was undeniably God's establishment. Paul solidifies this fact in his reference of the Covenant between man and woman when he said, "…as the woman is "of the man", even so is the man also "by the woman", but **all things of God**" (1Cor:11:12). He's declaring that marriage is of God, and that it's by His design. And since it is "*of God*," it carriers the connotation that marriage is spiritual in both purpose and nature – and that it's holy and sanctified in every way! Because of this, *All Rights are Reserved by God! And no one – not in society, nor it's government has the authority to change, or make any provisions or alterations. Those who infringe upon the rights reserved by God in His original design, will also be subject to His judgment!

> *Prov:14:34-35*
>
> *Righteousness exalteth a nation: but sin is a reproach to any people. The King's favour is toward a wise servant: but his wrath is against him that causeth shame. KJV*

Chapter 3

The Structure of Marriage

Marriages patterned after God's design are marriages that have the foundation and the framework (structure) of the Word of God. The objective of the design is to bless, honor and glorify God, while giving glorious revelation to the mystery of His love, character and oneness that could not otherwise be known by man any other way! The DNA for God's original design for marriage is found in the union of Adam and his wife in the Garden of Eden. The design reveals the Will of God for all committed Covenant relationships between husband and wife.

God established the Covenant to be exclusively between "one man" and "one woman" until death. Obviously, we see a number of variations in the world today. But this doesn't omit, negate nor override God's original plan or design. It's up to every believer and lover of God to hold-fast to what is true (which is outlined in His Word)! If a person does not believe, nor respect the Word of God, then we cannot expect them to honor God and hold His Word as true for their lives. Nonetheless, God expects every true believer to take a firm stance on His Word without wavering (*Rom:3:3-4*) just as He does!

Many argue that times have changed, and so does people and their views – and that might be so… But God and His Word NEVER changes for anything or anyone!

Heb:13:8

Jesus Christ the same yesterday, and to day, and for ever.

KJV

Mal:3:6

For I am the LORD, I change not; therefore ye sons of Jacob are not consumed. KJV

Ps:119:89

"For ever, O LORD, thy word is settled in heaven." KJV

Therefore, believers in Christ should never be found swaying back and forth on things they know to be true, nor changing their views to favor anything that clearly opposes the Word of God (*Rom:12:2; Jms:1:5-8*).

The Scriptures are very clear that God never intended the same gender to participate in an intimate, nor a Covenant relationship of marriage. It defeats the very purpose of its design. God purposely formed a "Woman" to be a suitable partner for Adam in every way. This appears even more evident when God gave them the charge to be fruitful and populate the earth. Same-sex partners are physically incapable of fulfilling this command. Because this command requires the two to intimately come together and create life.

As mentioned elsewhere, Genesis 2:23 says that when God brought "the helpmeet" to Adam so he could name her, he said "she shall be called *Woman*", because she was taken out of man. It's important to note that Adam said *"she"* (*and not he*) shall be called "Woman".

The name *Adam* meant *"man"*, so the name "Wo-man" would mean "*Adam* with a *womb, or man (i.e. mankind) with a womb.*" The first part of the Woman's name, "*Wo*" – gave designation to *the kind of human* that she was. She was of "*mankind*", but with a "*womb*", hence the term "*Wo-man*". Further, the term "*man*" as it relates to her name, *was not* referencing her *gender,* but rather *her nature* – meaning *of a man; or after man's likeness; or a member of the hu-man race* (hence, identifying *type of man,* and not *gender*). This is also how the term "female" relates to gender. It describes one made in the likeness *of a human male,* but created with the *necessary reproductive structure* to carry *a fetus,* hence the term "*Fe-male*".

There is absolutely no Scriptural evidence that God ever condoned intimate relationships, or marriages between the same-gender. This is not said to "quote-unquote," gay-bash, nor to spread some sort of hate message by any means! This is said simply to point out God's original design for marriage according to "the Holy Scriptures".

God absolutely loves "the people" who are caught-up in homosexual lifestyles, but He absolutely hates "the sin" of homosexuality, and God is calling them out of "the sin". We cannot say we love everyone by turning a blind-eye to the kind of behavior that will put them in jeopardy of God's judgment. It's love that warns of the coming judgment and destruction that lies ahead. And throughout Biblical history, God has always met rebellious and perverted behaviors/lifestyles with judgment upon those who refuse to heed His warnings. Moses communicated God's feelings on this topic under the law when he wrote:

Lev:20:13:

If a man also lie with mankind, as he lieth with a woman, both of them have committed an abomination: they shall surely be put to death; their blood shall be upon them. KJV

Paul also conveying a similar warning to the Church at Rome concerning those societies who have turned from following God:

Rom:1:26-28

For this cause God gave them up unto vile affections: for even their women did change the natural use into that which is against nature: And likewise also the men, leaving the natural use of the woman, burned in their lust one toward another; men with men working that which is unseemly, and receiving in themselves that recompence of their error which was meet. And even as they did not like to retain God in their knowledge, God gave them over to a reprobate mind, to do those things which are not convenient;

These warnings are not just to the homosexual community, but they are for everyone who crosses those boundaries that have been set by God (as mentioned in Chapter 2). The Scriptures conclude over and over again, that God designed 'the structure of marriage' to be exclusively between "one man" and "one woman".

> Gen:1:27-28
>
> *So God created man in his own image, in the image of God created he him;* **male** *and* **female** *created he them. And God blessed them, and God said unto them,* **Be fruitful***, and* **multiply***, and* **replenish** *the earth, and subdue it... KJV*

> Gen:5:1-2
>
> *This is the book of the generations of Adam. In the day that God created man, in the likeness of God made he him;* **Male** *and* **female** *created he them;* **and blessed them***, and called their name Adam, in the day when they were created. KJV*

> Jesus also confirming this in Mk:10:6-9
>
> *But* **from the beginning** *of the creation God made them* **male** *and* **female***.* **For this cause** *(For what cause? For the cause of marriage; Covenant) shall a man leave his*

*father and mother, and cleave to **his wife**; And they twain (or two) shall be **one flesh**: so then they are **no more twain** but **one flesh** (they are no longer two individuals, but one body comprised). What therefore **God hath joined** together, let not man put asunder.* KJV

Chapter 4

The Purpose of Marriage

While there may be many assumptions about God's objective for marriage, the true purpose of marriage cannot be understood until the relationship aligns with the framework of God's Word. It's only then that one could truly comprehend *the mysteries* of God's *love* and *Oneness* He has with them as *a redeemed people or church.*

Eph:5:30-32

*For **we are members** of **his body**, of **his flesh**, and of **his bones**. For this cause shall a man leave his father and mother,* *and shall be joined unto his wife, and they two shall be one flesh. This is **a great mystery**: but I speak concerning **Christ** and **the church**. KJV*

The Reality of God's Love

Many relationships are founded upon an emotional love; a love that is based on feelings. But emotions are merely a by-product of genuine love! Love causes the emotions to respond, react or feel, but those feelings are not to be confused with *"love itself"*. Those are just our emotion's *response to love*. And if we do not understand what *real love* is, then as our feelings change, so does our *'response or reaction'* to the one we say we love. This is where we get the term "infatuation". Infatuation is a strong, but short-lived *liking of someone* that is often confused with love. It's a surface or shallow kind of *emotional love*; it's inconsistent and unstable. But real love – the kind of love that God has towards us and that He desires to reveal in marriages, is everlasting, unconditional, and is a self-sacrificing kind of love.

Eph:5:25-29

*Husbands, love your wives, even **as Christ** also **loved** the church, and **gave himself** for it; That he might sanctify and cleanse it with the washing of water by the word, That he might present it to himself a glorious church, not having spot, or wrinkle, or any such thing; but that it should be holy and without blemish. **So ought men to love their wives** as their own bodies. He that loveth his wife loveth himself. For no man ever yet hated his own flesh; but nourisheth and cherisheth it, even as the Lord the church. KJV*

There are several words in the *Greek* that are used for the English word "love". There is *"Eros"*, meaning "a passionate kind of love"; mostly sexual in nature; having sensual desire and longing. Then there is *"Philia"*, which is a general type of love – a friendship kind of love; a love that usually exists between family members, friends, or it can be expressed about the enjoyment of an activity. *Storgē* is the word that translates the kind of love that conveys natural affection or empathy as between a parent and a child; the understanding and sharing through a mental or emotional connection. But then there's *Agapē* – which is "love unconditional". Love that cannot be earned; it's a love that is undeserved. *Agapē* is a self-sacrificing kind of love.

The Key Characteristics of Agapē

Paul expounds upon God's *Agapē* by outlining some of its key characteristics in his letter to the Church at Corinth. Though he uses the term "charity", charity is translated as the "*Agapē*" kind of love (see *1Cor:13:4-8*):

1Cor:13:4

- ✓ *Agapē* suffers long – meaning "love is patient"
- ✓ *Agapē* is kind; entreating; non-threating
- ✓ *Agapē* is not envious of the object of its affection; it doesn't allow us to feel resentful or at a disadvantage
- ✓ "Charity vaunteth not itself; it's not puffed up" – *Agapē* does not boast or brag; it doesn't seize the opportunity to capitalize on someone's weakness. It's not proud or arrogant; it's not afraid to apologize or to admit wrong

Verse:5

- ✓ *Agapē* does not behave itself unseemly; *Agapē* is not rude
- ✓ *Agapē* seeks not her own; it's not self-seeking or selfish – having the attitude, "What's in it for me?"
- ✓ *Agapē* is not easily provoked; it's not easily angered
- ✓ *Agapē* thinks no evil (assumes "good-will" or good intentions)
- ✓ *Agapē* keeps no record of wrongs; its forgiving; it gives the benefit of the doubt

Verse:6

- ✓ *Agapē* rejoices not in iniquity, but rejoices in the truth; it doesn't delight in evil, but rejoices in what is right; *Agapē* works no ill towards its neighbor (*see also Rom:13:10*)

Verse:7

- ✓ *Agapē* bears all things; it always protects; it always covers (*see also 1Pt:4:8*)
  - ❖ *Agapē* will shield, guard against; encamps or surround; as in providing safety

- ❖ *Agapē* says, "I will not expose you – I will protect you"
- ✓ *Agapē* believes all things; it always finds a way to trust
- ✓ *Agapē* hopeth all things; it always expects a good outcome
- ✓ *Agapē* endures all things; it always perseveres

Verse:8

- ✓ *Agapē* never faileth
  - ❖ *Agapē* says, "I will never let you down; you can always count on me"

Agapē loves even in the absence of love, or when the object of love does not have the capacity to love you back:

Rom:5:6-8

For when we were yet without strength, in due time Christ died for the ungodly. For scarcely for a righteous man will one die: yet peradventure for a good man some would even dare to die. But God commendeth (demonstrated) his love toward us, in that, while we were yet sinners, Christ died for us. KJV

Agapē Reveals Character

The Greek word for "character" is *kharaktēr* – it was a stamping tool, used to give something a distinctive mark. Character can then be defined as a complex of attributes that determines a person's moral and/or ethical actions and reactions. The Apostle John makes a profound statement in 1John:4:8, he says that *"God is Love"*! Denoting that "God is One with His character; He IS the full manifestation of *Agapē* Love". Which is to say that *not only* does God *"demonstrate His love"*, but His love is a *"distinctive mark"* that signifies Who He is "by" what He does!

1Jn:3:16-18

Hereby perceive we **the love of God**, *because he* **laid down his life for us**: *and* **we ought to lay down our lives for the brethren**. *But whoso hath this world's good, and seeth his brother have need, and shutteth up his bowels of compassion from him,* **how dwelleth** *the love of God in him? My little* *children, let us not love in word, neither in tongue; but **in deed** and **in truth**. KJV*

In other words, love should be a *"distinctive mark"* for every believer, and even more so, for a husband and wife. Our actions should, and do define who we truly are (denoting our character) which signifies our makeup!

As we endeavor to grow in God's *Agapē*, the Holy Spirit will mature us, and produce in us the very same characteristics that He possess, which we now know as "the fruit of the Spirit":

Gal:5:22-23

…the fruit of the Spirit is love, joy, peace, longsuffering, gentleness, goodness, faith, meekness, temperance: against such there is no law. KJV

Eph:5:9-10

…For the fruit of the Spirit is in all goodness and righteousness and truth; Proving what is acceptable unto the Lord. KJV

Chapter 5

The Mystery of Oneness

God uses Covenant to give revelation to the mystery of oneness. Covenant is as much a spiritual agreement, as it is a contractual agreement. Which is to say that – anything we enter into an agreement with, *a spiritual bond* takes place making us *"one"* with that thing. "Our agreement" unites us spiritually in a Covenant, making us members of the same body.

Paul explains this in 1Corinthains Chapter 15 as he addresses the sin of fornication. He first establishes the fact that the believer is "one-body" with Christ! And using a harlot as an example, he demonstrates that if a believer engages in sexual sin with her, then he's taking the members of Christ (which is his body) and joining them to, or uniting them with a harlot. The believer's behavior *expresses agreement* with the source (which is *fornication, or sexual immorality*), thereby making him "*one* or *one body*" with it in Covenant.

> 1Cor:6:15-17
>
> *Know ye not that your bodies are the members of Christ? shall I then take the members of Christ, and make them the members of an harlot? God forbid. What? know ye not that he which is joined to an harlot is one body? for two, saith he, shall be one flesh. But he that is joined unto the Lord is one spirit.*
>
> 2Cor:6:14-17
>
> *Be ye not unequally yoked together with unbelievers (again, the underlining message here is agreement – agreement yokes you together in Covenant): for what fellowship hath righteousness with unrighteousness?*

and what communion hath light with darkness? And what concord hath Christ with Belial? or what part hath he that believeth with an infidel? And what "agreement" hath the temple of God with idols? for ye are the temple of the living God; as God hath said, I will dwell in them, and walk in them; and I will be their God, and they shall be my people. Wherefore come out from among them, and be ye separate, saith the Lord, and touch not the unclean thing; and I will receive you,

So, God calls us out from among the ungodly things, because our *affiliation* with them expresses agreement, and our agreement unites us in Covenant, and we essentially become *members of the same body* through our agreement.

What's amazing to discover is that Adam fully understood Covenant relationship even as he related it to him and his wife. I know that for years, children's books, movies and cartoons have historically portrayed the first man and woman as naïve, simple and/or uneducated beings, who had about as much knowledge as new born babes. But,

Adam and his wife were some extremely intelligent human beings.

Although they were innocent, they were far from naïve. The Bible gives us to understand that they were both created perfect; they were both created in the image and likeness of God! And being that God is Omniscient, which means that He possesses all wisdom, knowledge and understanding – I think it would be safe to say, that if God created them in His own image and likeness, then He would've also given them a *great deal of wisdom, knowledge* and *understanding,* especially if they were given *absolute authority* and commanded to *govern* the whole world! After all, we would expect for world leaders today to have a great deal of education before considering the office in just one nation or state (i.e. the office of the president, or some other public office).

So wouldn't it be reasonable to think that if God gave them such a charge (especially after knowing beforehand how great the world would become), that He would've also given them extensive knowledge and comprehension of the world that they would rule.

Gen:1:26-28

And God said, Let us make man in our image, after our likeness: and let them have dominion over the fish of the sea, and over the fowl of the air, and over the cattle, and over all the earth, and over every creeping thing that creepeth upon the earth. So God created man in his own image, in the image of God created he him; male and female created he them (as one flesh). And God blessed them (as one flesh), and God said unto them (as one flesh), Be fruitful, and multiply, and replenish the earth, and subdue it: and have dominion over the fish of the sea, and over the fowl of the air, and over every living thing that moveth upon the earth. KJV

It's also important to point-out that the wisdom, knowledge and understanding that they had was not the kind that comes from the Textbooks of man, but they were created with the Mind of God. So, I would venture to even say that *not only* were they intelligent, but they were *"super intelligent"* human beings – with knowledge greater than any doctors, physicists, mathematicians or computer scientists known to mankind today!

With this in mind – let's examine Adam's response after God made the Woman from one of his ribs? When God brought her to him to see what he would call her, Adam having "full understanding" of what God had done – he profoundly states, "This is NOW bone of my bones, and flesh of my flesh: she shall be called Woman, BECAUSE she was taken OUT OF MAN".

Just as a sidebar: notice that *she* was to be called *"Woman,"* and *not he,* and *not Eve.* The name *"Eve"* was not given to her until *"after the fall"* through disobedience in the garden (*see, Gen:3:19-20*).

But *"before the fall"*, she was called *"Woman"* (which means, *mankind with a womb*). Adam took note of her features and understood that everything about her was for Covenant purposes: i.e. he is the head and she is a member of his body; his external complies with her internal; he produces the seed and she gives birth to the seed and etc.

Since Adam understood the Mind of God, he did not see he and his wife as two separate individuals, but saw themselves as "one-flesh" in the same way that God did! He saw themselves as "members of the same body" – so he said, "This is NOW bone of my bones, and flesh of my flesh: she shall be called Woman, BECAUSE she was taken OUT OF MAN – Therefore (or because of this; because woman was taken out of man) shall *every* man *entering into marriage* leave his father and mother, and shall cleave (*or be joined*) unto his wife: and they shall be ONE FLESH; or members of the same body (Gen:2:23-24)."

Before the fall, God did not acknowledge them by two separate names, but He called them by *"one name"*, Adam. However God saw the head, is how He saw the body also, because the head is fully responsible for his own body.

Gen:5:1-2
This is the book of the generations of Adam. In the day that God created man, in the likeness of God made he

*him; Male and female created he them; and blessed them, and called **their name** Adam, in the day when they were created. KJV*

This original design for marriage between Adam and his wife gives revelation to *"the oneness"* that we (as the Church) have with Christ. In the same way that God did not view the Woman separately from Adam – God does not view the Church separate from Christ! WHY? Because we are in Covenant with Him; we are one-body in Christ! So, however God sees the Head, is how He see the body also, because the Head is fully responsible for His own body.

Eph:5:23
For the husband is the head of the wife, even as Christ is the head of the church: and he is the saviour of the body (denoting full responsibility).

God views us as one-flesh with Christ! Our agreement that He is the Son of God unites us with God's plan of redemption through His blood; our agreement that He is the

Savior unites us in Covenant as heirs of God, and joint-heirs with Christ (Rom:8:17); our acceptance means that we agree with God; it's through our admission that we agree with the Source (Who is God).

Further, our obedience is "a sign or a symbol" of our acceptance! If we obey His Word, then we're declaring in agreement that His Word is true. Otherwise, why would we willfully obey something or someone that we do not agree with? Our agreement unites us in Covenant; brings us into fellowship, and declares that we are one; that we are members of the same body!

> *Eph:5:30-32*
>
> *For we are members of his body, of his flesh, and of his bones. For this cause shall a man leave his father and mother, and shall be joined unto his wife, and they two shall be one flesh. This is a great mystery: but I speak concerning Christ and the church.*

Because of our Covenant with Christ, God doesn't see us as the ungodly sinners that we use to be, but He see us the same way He see our Head, Who is Christ (*1Cor:6:9-11*)! And God calls us by *"one Name"*, *"Jesus Christ"* – even as He did Adam and his wife (Gen:5:1-2).

Jn:1:10-12

*He was in the world, and the world was made by him, and the world knew him not. He came unto his own, and his own received him not. But as many as received him, to them gave he **power to become** the **sons of God**, even to them that **believe on his name**.*

Jn:20:31

*But these are written, that ye might believe that Jesus is the Christ, the Son of God; and that believing ye might have life **through his name**. KJV*

Mt:28:18-20

*And Jesus came and spake unto them, saying, All power is given unto me in heaven and in earth. Go ye therefore, and teach all nations, **baptizing them in the name** of the Father, and of the Son, and of the Holy Ghost:*

Teaching them to observe all things whatsoever I have commanded you: and, lo, I am with you alway, even unto the end of the world. Amen. KJV

Acts:2:38-39
Then Peter said unto them, Repent, and be baptized every one of you **in the name of Jesus Christ** *for the remission of sins, and ye shall receive the gift of the Holy Ghost. For the promise is unto you, and to your children, and to all that are afar off, even as many as the Lord our God shall call. KJV*

Baptism (*submersion*) in the Name identifies you with *the One* to whom you're in Covenant with. Paul explains that the fathers (*or their ancestors – the Israelites*) were all baptized unto Moses when they were under the cloud, and all passed through the sea (1Cor:10:1-4) – denoting that the experience connected them to the Covenant and provisions that were given by the hand of Moses. Further, those who receive baptism from *John the Baptist* were "baptized by water unto repentance," identifying them *with John* and *the provisions* of "forgiveness of sins" while they were being made ready to accept "the coming Christ" (Isa:40:3-5 Mk:1:2-5; Mt:3:11-12). Likewise, baptism in the Name of Jesus identifies the believer with God's redemptive plan of Salvation through Christ. And gives us full access to all the promises and provisions that are included in the Covenant established by His blood (Lu:22:19-20; Rom:8:1-4; 1Cor:11:23-25; Heb:12:24).

So again, our obedience (as seen here in baptism) is *"a sign"* of our acceptance! And if we obey, we are declaring our agreement with His Word, which *spiritually joins us* to Christ.

> 1Cor:12:13
>
> *For by one Spirit are we all baptized into one body, whether we be Jews or Gentiles, whether we be bond or free; and have been all made to drink into one Spirit.*

Chapter 6

Singleness to Oneness

Singleness

A "Single" person is an individual who possess all the characteristics of being alone; all in one, or complete within themselves – very much like Adam was when he was first created.

During one of our Single's Conferences, Elder Tywana Chachere (*one of our Single ministers*) expounded saying: "Apart from being accountable to God, a Single person can virtually do whatever they want, whenever they want, and however they want to do it (of course, within their means and within reason). They require no one's permission for anything. They don't have to tell anyone where they're going, or what time they'll be back. They can spend as much of their own money as they want, without having to give an account to anyone else."

And that's so true! But when they marry, more than likely those liberties will change dramatically by virtue of the Covenant one is entering into! If the marriage is going to survive, then *"change"* is inevitable: change of mindset; change in priorities, and even possibly a change in future goals.

I've heard some wives say, in making reference to their husband, "I'm not going to lose myself *as an individual* for "anyone"! I'm *my own person*! I have *a life too*! I have *my own dreams, goals* and *aspirations*!" Unfortunately, if this is your view on marriage, then "marriage" is definitely *not for you*! Because "by God's design," that's exactly what God expect you to do in marriage. God expects you to form "one-life," which will require you to give-up quite-a-bit of who you are as an individual, if not all!

This is why it's so vitally important that you *take the time* to make a *good conscious decision* on who it is you're marrying. Additionally, this is why premarital counseling is so important – because *you need to know* who it is you're marrying? Is this who you really want to share the rest of your life with? Do you both share the same thoughts and desires as a family and for the future?

Wives *need to be able* to answer questions like – is this someone I'm willing to *submit to*, and *entrust my future to* as God requires? Am I willing to *submit to his authority* as my husband? Am I willing to *trust in his leadership* for our household? Can I trust that *he will seek to hear* from *God* for our family? Can I *trust* that *this man will love me* and *care for me* the way the Bible instructs and commands him to?

Husbands *need to be able* to answer questions like – is this someone *I am willing to love* as Christ also loved the church? Am I willing to *love her unconditionally*? Am I willing to *give myself* for her (meaning, to put her as *the highest priority* in my life under God, even if it means *sacrificing my own personal needs, desires* and *dreams* for her wellbeing)? Am I willing to *be patient* with her; *longsuffering* with her? Do I believe that *this woman* will *respect me, honor me* and *submit to me* as her husband the way the Bible instructs her to?

If you are unable to truthfully answer these questions: (1) marriage may not be for you, or (2) this may not be the person for you. Too often, a couples' decision is clouded with infatuation and they do not answer truthfully. But if you choose to marry without having made a good assessment, or if you marry having overlooked the obvious, GOD WILL STILL hold you accountable to that marriage and expect you to honor your vow before Him! Therefore, it behooves us to make a well-thought-out decision concerning this lifetime commitment:

1Cor:7:39:

The wife is bound by the law as long as her husband liveth… KJV

As we can see, God views marriage much more seriously than society does. Society believes that marriage is a breakable Covenant, but God sees it as a everlasting commitment; a commitment so strong that only death can free you from it! So, IF WE CHOOSE TO (keeping in mind that marriage is a choice), God will honor our decision – but we are literally voiding-out our life as *an individual* and *agreeing* to *take-on* and *share* a *new life* with someone else. Thereby, God will no longer see our identity as *a Single* person – but He'll view us as "*one-flesh*" with our spouse!

Gen:2:24

Therefore shall a man leave his father and his mother, and shall cleave unto his wife: and they shall be one flesh. KJV

Single, but Celibate

There are only a select few who have been given the "*gift of grace*" to live Single, but celibate lives. Those who are able to control the cravings and appetites of their flesh – the Bible refers to them as "Eunuchs". A Eunuch is defined by Webster as a man or boy deprived of the testes or external genitals; one who is castrated. But the spiritual implication is that it refers to one having no need of sex, or one having no trouble in the flesh (which implies "the cutting-off" of the desire).

In Mk:10:11-12, Jesus said:

...All men cannot receive this saying, save (or except) they to whom it is given. For there are some eunuchs, which were so born from their mother's womb: and there are some eunuchs, which were made eunuchs of men: and there be eunuchs, which have made themselves eunuchs for the kingdom of heaven's sake. He that is able to receive it, let him receive it. KJV

In the spiritual sense, it appears that Paul made himself such a Eunuch for the Kingdom's sake:

Paul said in 1Cor:7:7-8:

*For I would (prefer) that **all men** were **even as I myself**. But **every man** hath **his proper gift** of God, one after this manner, and another after that. I say therefore to **the unmarried** (Singles) and **widows** (previously married, but now Single), It is good for them if they abide **even as I**. KJV*

1Cor:9:3-5:

*Mine answer to them that do examine me is this, Have we not power to eat and to drink? Have we not **power to lead about a sister, a wife**, as well **as other apostles**, and **as the brethren** of the Lord, and Cephas? KJV*

Marriage is a Choice

Paul said that he has every right to marry just like anyone else does, but he simply *chose not to* for the Gospel's sake! Some are searching for Mr. or Mrs. "right"; some are seeking the Lord, praying that He would send them their special mate; some are praying "Lord, if it be Your Will for me, let it be." And that's all good! We should pray about everything, especially something as serious as marriage. But Biblically, God leaves "*the choice*" up to us to marry! Even if He brought the perfect person in our lives, God leaves the final decision for us to make, because He EXPECTS us to honor the commitment that He requires in marriage!

Let's understand this – if marriage *was not* a choice, and God was to choose for us rather we should marry or not, we would probably all be "Single"! This way, we can devote all of our time and attention to Him and to His service (1Cor:7:32). But the reality is, God leaves this decision to us! If we choose to marry, then God expects us to honor the Covenant we've made with our spouse so that we may serve Him together as "one", and not be divided in our hearts struggling with the flesh.

I think it would be safe to say that it's God's *preference* for us to be "single", but it's His *Will* for us to be "whole". Which is the difference between "Singleness" and "Oneness". Meaning that God would prefer that we were *Single (as Paul stated in 1Cor:7:7)*, but it would be *more beneficial to us* to be *One* (or whole; undivided; complete through marriage)!

God would rather us to be *alone*; all in one; or complete within ourselves (*if we could handle it as a Single*), because then, He could be the Object of our *devotion*. But if sexual urges develop into *struggles in the flesh*, it's likely that a person will eventually become double-minded, divided within themselves and cannot focus on what's most important, which is their relationship with God. Although they may "want to focus" on God's plan and Will for their lives, "*they can't*" because they are distracted by the lust that's *waging war* within their flesh.

This is obviously Paul's point to the church at Corinth on the topic of Singleness and marriage:

In 1Cor:7:1, Paul says:
It is good for a man not to touch a woman (to remain celibate). Nevertheless, to avoid fornication, let every man have his own wife, and let every woman have her own husband. KJV

He goes on to say in Verse:7: that he'd rather that everyone was Single even as he is, But *if they cannot contain* (Verse:9), "let them marry: for it is better to marry than to burn." Some have supposed that Paul was suggesting that "it is better to marry than to burn in hell". But he was actually saying that "it's better to marry than to burn with passion, desire or flaming lust." WHY? Because it will keep you divided in your heart toward God, and may eventually lead to sin.

He also gives these same instructions to those who are in dating relationships where there may be no sexual interaction involved – he says that if you find yourself where you *cannot contain* or *control* your sexual desires, *"Let them marry!"*

> 1Cor:7:36-37:
>
> *But if any man think that he behaveth himself uncomely toward his virgin, if she pass the flower of her age (if she is of age), and need so require, let him do what he will, he sinneth not: let them marry. Nevertheless he that standeth stedfast in his heart, having no necessity, but hath power over his own will, and hath so decreed in his heart that he will keep his virgin, doeth well. KJV*

These passages validate the fact that God would *prefer* us to be *"single"*, but His *Will* for us is to be "whole!" We know that *"love"* is very important to the success of any marriage, but as important as love is, Paul didn't say, "if they love each other, let them marry…" He said, *"to avoid fornication, let them marry…"* Denoting the *"importance of your relationship with Him*"; being in right-standing with Him far more supersedes any other reason for marriage! That it's more important for you to maintain "a right-relationship" with Him – than to sin in your heart being distracted by lust, or to physically commit the sin of fornication.

But again, "marriage is a choice" that God allows us to make. And if a person makes "the choice" to marry, God will gladly honor and bless the union. But He intends for us to enter into the commitment well-aware of WHAT HE EXPECTS from us as believers!

The Process of Becoming One

Marriage consists of the complexity of two "individual lives" coming together to form "one-life" in harmony. More often than not, these individuals are bringing into the relationship (1) two completely different backgrounds (one may come from a home with both parents, while the other may come from a broken home); (2) two different upbringings (one may have been taught that the husband is the sole provider and "the wife's place" is at home – while the other may have been taught that the husband and wife are equal partners and are equally responsible for their financial contributions to the home); and (3) having different ideas or concepts of marriage and family; they may have different thoughts of how it should function or operate. And these lives must be fashioned together and form one life; to function as a single unit.

To do so, they must both be willing to "*drop their identities*" as *individuals* and strive to become "*one*" under the authority of God's Word! When a couple marries, it's no longer about them "*as an individual*" or about their "*individual lives*", but they are making a conscience decision to embrace their *roles* and *responsibilities* within the relationship as outlined by God *to unify* and *live as one*. They must transition from a *Single mindset* to a *mindset* that makes them *One*!

A couple's ability to "*agree*" can become one of the greatest tools to aid them in becoming "*one!*" Agreement promotes "*oneness,*" and it helps to bring you *out of the mindset* that your life and decisions are just about you.

Amos:3:3

Can two walk together, except they be agreed? KJV

If the goal is to be together, then there must be an agreement! Agreement does not mean that you will always see things eye-to-eye. There may be times when you'll have to agree by compromising, or yielding to the decision of your spouse – letting them take the lead on a particular issue. In that sense, you may not be agreeing on the way it's being handled, but you are agreeing to trust them with the decision, while you support them on it. And as long as the decision doesn't violate the Word of God, it'll all be ok!

One final note, while agreement is essential, we must keep in mind God's order. The husband's position in the marriage is the headship role, which means that God has given him the authority to make the final decision. And whatever decision he makes, rather it's good or bad, God is holding him fully accountable and responsible for that decision! Equally important to note, the wife is God's gift to her husband! God has Anointed her to be his *"helper!"* So, as it is wise of good leadership to seek the counsel of other good leaders when making important decisions, it's also wise for husbands to consider counsel or advice of his wife – because that's who she's Anointed to be in his life!

Chapter 7

Vision for Marriage

"Vision" is essential to every successful institution or organization! It helps to promote cohesion, camaraderie and oneness among everyone involved! Vision provides sight, direction and an expectation to what is hoped to be gained. Vision gives a visual snap-shot or a mental image of the objective, and it's especially important to Covenant relationships.

Prov:29:18:

Where there is no vision, the people perish (lit. cast off restraints): but he that keepeth the law, happy is he.

Solomon gives this insight, "when people have no Vision, they tend to live lawlessly (or cast off restraints)." Which means that they wander without direction; they are subject to transgress or go beyond boundaries that should keep them safe. But he says, "happy" (lit. *blessed*) is the one who keeps the law (*obeys God's Word*); keeps the way; or stay on the course.

Since marriage is "God's own design", wisdom would tell us that Vision for marriage would come from Him. If anyone would know how to get the best out of marriage, it would be God, the One Who established it!

Jer:29:11:

For I know the thoughts that I think toward you, saith the LORD, thoughts of peace, and not of evil, to give you an expected end. KJV

This passage tells us that God has "thoughts" towards each of us; a plan and an expectation for peace in every area of our lives. The term *"Thought"* is one of several interpretations of the Greek word *"logos"* (which is lit. "Word" in its English form). So, if we were to swap this translation in Jeremiah's passage – it could read, "I know the *Word* I've spoken concerning you!" And there is a Word that produces God's Vision for our relationships; a Word that gives us a snap-shot of what the end-result should look like, and a Word that gives a clear path on how to accomplish it in our marriages. We simply have to turn to Him for the plan, the guidance, and the instructions.

The Bible teaches that God is a *"God of order"* – and He design marriage with a particular organizational structure. A structure that Corporate America have adopted that contributed to the success of many companies for decades. An organizational structure that consists of a Founder, a Vision, an institution, and key leaders.

When a person is hired for a job, the first thing that most companies do is take the employee through orientation. The orientation usually introduces the employee to the founder(s) of the company; the history of the company; the company's Vision, and the chain of command (or key leaders). This is done to orientate and unify the new employee with the company, and to set them on course to achieving the company's Mission and Vision.

Being that many of us can identify with this scenario, we should be able to relate to God's structure for the family:

1Cor:11:3

...I would have you know, that the head of every man is Christ; and the head of the woman is the man; and the head of Christ is God. KJV

The phrase "the head" denotes the lead position. It can be better understood as *an authority figure* who is *overall accountable* and *responsible* for the members of his own body.

This would mean that, (1) God is *the authority figure* for Christ, and He is *overall accountable* and *responsible* for His own body (which is Christ) – in the days of His flesh, Jesus was incarnate and became the human body of the invisible God, or the visible image of the invisible God (Jn:1:1&14;

Jn:14:8-9; Col:1:15; Heb:10:5-7), (2) Christ is *the authority figure* for the man, because by virtue of *his position* in the family, the man is a *direct representation* of Christ's role to the Church. Therefore, Christ is *overall accountable* and *responsible* for the man who represents His body, and (3) the man is *the authority figure* for the woman, and is *overall accountable* and *responsible* for the members of his own body, which is his family.

> *Eph:5:23*
>
> *For the husband is the head of the wife, **even as** Christ is the head of the church: and he is the saviour of (His Own) body.*

Vision comes from the Founder of the organization. The Founder clearly understands the purpose for which the institution was formed. And he sets key leaders in place to help guide and accomplish certain aspects of the Vision. Paul says the following concerning *the Church*:

> *1Cor:12:18:*

> *"...God set the members every one of them in the body, as it hath pleased him."* KJV

But when we understand that the *husband/wife relationship* is simply *a picture* or *a direct representation* of Christ's relationship with the Church, then we'll understand that this passage applies to marriages as well. Just as the Church is a type of body, the family is also a type of body! And God set the members in the marriage (*or body*) as it pleased Him. This means that God knew exactly who He was assigning each role to in the family, as well as the responsibilities that accompany each role – and we have to learn to honor and appreciate them!

Although many may desire to lead, we know that *not everyone* can lead. Nonetheless, it takes as much strength, integrity and character *"to follow"* as it does *"to lead"*. Antonio Banderas made a very profound statement in one of his movies when he said, *"To follow, you must give your partner permission to lead you."* He was referring to dancing, but I thought, *"how adequately does this speaks to marriages!"* We must never feel slighted or insignificant in our roles, because every position God assigned to the family is vitally important (1Cor:12:15-18)!

According to 1Cor:11:3, the flow of the Vision for each family should come from God, to Christ, to the husband, then to the wife. This means that it's necessary for the husband to be in a position to be able to hear from his Head, which is Christ. Once the husband gets the Vision, he can then convey it to his wife so she can come along side and undergird the Vision God has given them.

These exact same principles are discovered in the Garden of Eden between Adam and his wife. Somewhere within the span of time when God created the Garden and He formed the Woman, the Bible says the following –

> *Gen:2:15-17*
>
> *...the LORD God took the man, and **put him into the garden** of Eden **to dress it** and **to keep it**. And the LORD God **commanded the man**, saying, **Of every tree of the garden thou mayest freely eat: But of the tree of the knowledge of good and evil, thou shalt**

not eat of it: for in the day that thou eatest thereof thou shalt surely die. *KJV*

God first gave Adam a purpose and a law (or command) in the Garden, *afterward* He made the Woman and brought her to him. It's obvious that Adam was *responsible* for communicating the "quote/unquote" *Vision* to his wife (the plan; their function and/or responsibility in the Garden), because nowhere does it state that God came a second time and gave the command to the Woman. But, we find her answering the Serpent in like manner:

Gen:3:1-3

Now the serpent was more subtil than any beast of the field which the LORD God had made. And he said unto the woman, Yea, **hath God said, Ye shall not eat of every tree of the garden?** *And* **the woman said** *unto the serpent,* **We may eat of the fruit of the trees of the garden: But of the fruit of the tree which is in the midst of the garden, God hath said, Ye shall not**

> *eat of it, neither shall ye touch it, lest ye die. KJV*

Some have said that this is not exactly what God told Adam, because it has more details then what we read initially in Gen:2:15-17. But I believe she said exactly what was communicated to her! And although she fell for the temptation, it's clear that she understood exactly what they were commanded to do and not to do!

Similarly, Christ communicates the Vision for every Church to the Pastor or Ministry Leader. The Leader is then responsible for casting the Vision to the subordinate leaders, and they in turn rally around the Vision to help see it through!

> *Eph:4:11-12 says that He gave gifts to the church:*
> *...He gave some, apostles; and some, prophets; and some, evangelists; and some, pastors and teachers" (denoting offices of leadership in the church). For the perfecting of the saints, for the work of the ministry, for the edifying of the body of Christ. KJV*

The study of Christ's relationship with the Church will give in-depth revelation to God's design for every godly marriage.

> *Eph:5:30-32:*
>
> *For we are members of his body, of his flesh, and of his bones. For this cause shall a man leave his father and mother, and shall be joined unto his wife, and they two shall be one flesh. This is a great mystery: but I speak concerning Christ and the church. KJV*

Vision will call for agreement – which means being unified and being of the same mind. There must be a constant endeavor to agree in spite of the many challenges that can arise! Everyone who is essential to the Vision must be in agreement in order for it to be a success as God intends!

Chapter 8

Roles & Responsibilities in Marriage

For years, Christian marriages have used Ephesians Chapter 5 as a sort of weapon to beat each other over the head to validate and establish their points while arguing over issues or pointing out the other person's inadequacies. For example: When there's a heated discussion over the bills, the wife might say – "Well, you're the head! THAT'S your responsibility!" Or, if the wife is over-talking him during the discussion, the husband might say, "You DON'T listen woman, you're supposed to SUBMIT! SUBMIT woman, SUBMIT!" It's funny now, but my wife and I used to have those same conversations!

But God never intended for Ephesians Chapter 5 to be a weapon of battle – unless you're using it against Satanic attacks against your home! On the contrary, it's not a weapon to tare each other down, but a tool to build your marriage into a habitation for God's glory to reside. Another way of looking at it – it's the perfect picture of how Christian marriages are supposed to look! It's the framework, or the pattern, or the blueprint for marriages to reflect the glory of God in their relationship! In other words, when you envision the marriage that is outlined in Ephesians Chapter 5, you're seeing exactly what God intended marriage to look like from the beginning!

Grant it, many of our marriages do not currently look like this! But that's ok, because they can! God has taken out the guesswork and has clearly mapped-out the roles and responsibilities for every member involved. And the underlining message of Ephesians Chapter 5 is – if you want a healthy, growing and successful marriage, then this is how to achieve it! And the mystery of "oneness" is revealed as your responses begin to resemble the relationship between Christ and the Church (*which is His bride*).

> *Eph:5:23-25*
>
> *For the husband is the head of the wife, **even as Christ** is the head of the church: and he is the saviour of the body. Therefore **as the church** is subject unto Christ, **so let the wives** be to their own husbands in every thing. Husbands, love your wives, **even as Christ** also loved the church, and gave himself for it. KJV*

The Role and Responsibilities of the Husband

In this framework, the husband's position or role is to portray that of Christ's Role to the Church. As Christ is the Head of the Church, so has God placed the husband as "the head" of the home. The headship role is one that assumes FULL responsibility for EVERYTHING! The rise or fall; sink or swim; success or failure of the "whole" falls totally upon the headship role in which God will hold him fully accountable! As Christ is FULLY responsible for His Church, the husband is FULLY responsible for his wife, his children and their success or failures!

Notice in Eph:5:23: "...Christ IS the HEAD *of the church*: and HE IS the SAVIOR *of the body.*" Which means He's FULLY RESPONSIBLE for the church, and His responsibility is to SAVE (or rescue) the body, of which your wife is part of yours!

Eph:5:28

So ought men to love their wives as their own bodies. He that loveth his wife loveth himself.

29 For no man ever yet hated his own flesh; but nourisheth and cherisheth it, even as the Lord the church. KJV

The ancient rabbis commented that the woman did not come from the man's head to rule over him; nor from his feet to be his slave; but from his side, next to his heart, so that he would cherish her.

The term "husband" also carries the meaning "house-band". A house-band is a "band" that holds the entire house together. Which also lends to the concept of the husband being directly and fully responsible. As inadequate as he may feel within himself, the husband was BUILT FOR THIS! God has equipped him to take on this kind of load, even if he doesn't feel capable… If he looks to God, He will uphold him – because remember, Christ is his Head (*1Cor:11:3*). The wife however, WAS NOT BUILT to take on this kind of responsibility! Even women who have no husbands can find peace in the fact that God is their "House-band" – He will be there for them, and be their Covering until a husband takes on that role.

Though the role of the husband can be quite challenging sometimes, and even frustrating, we are never to take-out our frustrations on our wives. Christ never takes-out frustrations on the Church! But He's a problem-solver; He's a way-maker, and He always loves! And that's what He expects from us as husbands – to solve the problems; to find the solutions; and if it seems to be *no answer*, that's when you turn to Him Who is *"your Head"* (Jesus Christ) – because He's the One responsible for you!

But as husbands, we must consistently "love, and demonstrate love" to our wives, THIS IS OUR MINISTRY to them! That's how we serve them, through our love. Wives are designed to respond to the love of their husbands. Women are "Receivers", and that's spiritually, mentally and naturally – it's all a part of their make-up. So, when they receive love; when they KNOW that they're loved; when genuine *Agapē* love is given to them – their natural response is to reverence (*respect and honor*) and to yield in humble submission. These kinds of responses cannot be demanded of them, because then, they would not be genuine and heart-felt – but love (true *Agapē*) provokes, compels or influences these behaviors. The Church responds to God with reverence, sincerity and submission, because His love is revealed in Christ.

> *Jn:3:16-17*
>
> *…God so loved the world, that he gave his only begotten Son, that whosoever believeth in him should not perish, but have everlasting life. For God sent not his Son into the world to condemn the world; but that the world through him might be saved.*

1Jn:4:19

We love him, because he first loved us.

Eph:2:4-5

But God, who is rich in mercy, for his great love wherewith he loved us, even when we were dead in sins, hath quickened us together with Christ, (by grace ye are saved)...

Eph:5:25

Husbands, love your wives, even as Christ also loved the church, and gave himself for it; That he might sanctify and cleanse it with the washing of water by the word, That he might present it to himself a glorious church, not having spot, or wrinkle, or any such thing; but that it should be holy and without blemish.

In order to fulfill our role as husbands, we must die daily. Meaning that as Christ sacrificed His own life for the sake of the ones He loved, husbands must realize that "their life" is not their own anymore... When they assume the role as a husband, their life becomes "all about" the ones they love! It's now about the physical, mental and spiritual welfare of their family! The Scripture says, *"That he (Jesus) might sanctify and cleanse; and that He might present it to himself a glorious church"*. A couple of things to note: (1) this again speaks to Jesus' direct responsibility (*as well as that of the husband*), and (2) His presentation of the Church will reveal how-well He cared for the Church – and His goal is for it to be *a glorious church* for Himself. Likewise, the presentation of our families; or *how they are presented* to others reveals *how-well* they are cared for, and the direction *they* are going in life – which is a direct reflection of us as husbands (*because we bear the overall responsibility*).

> 1Cor:11:7b-9
>
> ...**the woman is the glory of the man.** *For the man is not of the woman; but the woman of the man. Neither was the man created for the woman; but the woman for the man.*

Christ's relationship to the Church reveals that He is our Provider (Heb:10:10-12; Phil:4:19; 1Cor:2:9-10); our Healer (1Pt:2:24; Jms:5:14-15); our Protector (1Cor:15:57; Phil:4:13; Rom:8:31-32); our Peace (Isa:9:6; Jn:14:27; Eph:2:14); our Shepherd Who leads, guides and directs (Jn:10:11 & 14).

In a similar fashion, the husband is the primary provider, protector, healer (*physically, spiritually and emotionally*), the shepherd who leads, guides and directs (Josh:24:15), and he's the primary "peace-maker, or the one who brings peace" to his family.

The Role and Responsibilities of the Wife

In the framework of marriage as outlined in Ephesians Chapter 5, the wife's position or role is to emulate "the Church's response" to Christ.

> *Eph:5:22*
> *Wives, submit yourselves unto your own husbands, as unto the Lord.*

Verse:24

Therefore as the church is subject unto Christ, so let the wives be to their own husbands in every thing.

Some women find the term "submit" offensive as it pertains to submitting to their husbands. But as you view it the way God does (*as shown in Eph:5:24*), submission is actually a place of blessing. In the same way the Church is in a place of blessing when they are submitted to Christ, wives are also in a place of blessing when they are submitted to their own husbands in everything (*it's Divine order*)! Notice that Verse:22 says to do it "as unto the Lord." In other words, do it out of obedience and reverence to God – because He placed the husband in that position, and gave him the authority to function as the head. Keep in mind that the same understanding that we have *of the Church* is to give revelation to our marriages:

1Cor:12:18:

"…God set the members every one of them in the body, as it hath pleased him." KJV

It's the Church's *acceptance* of Jesus as Savior, and their *submission to His leadership* as Lord that makes them part of His body. In the same way, it's wife's *acceptance* of her husband's role, and her *submission to his leadership* that makes her *a member* of his body.

God made the wife for the *primary purpose* of being a *help-meet* to her husband. Not to be *another head*, but a *"help-meet"*. This should actually be a *sigh of relief* to the wife to know that the burden of the overall responsibility of the headship role was placed upon the man, and that he is held *directly accountable* to God for the *success* or *failure* of the family. Now of course, there are those situations where he may not be held liable due to, perhaps the wife *not being submissive*, or *infidelity* is a factor – in such cases, God will judge.

The wife, *the help-meet's* responsibility is to come alongside of her husband and *"help"* him accomplish *God's Vision* for their lives. And I do STRESS the word *"help"*!

God does not expect the wife to assume FULL responsibility for the household! He does not intend for her to be the *"house-band,"* the one who holds the house together! It's not her primary responsibility to provide, protect or lead the family! Her job is to *"Help!"*

> 1Pet:3:7
>
> *Likewise, ye husbands, dwell with them according to knowledge, giving honour unto the wife, as unto **the weaker vessel**, and as being **heirs together** of the grace of life; that your prayers be not hindered.*

The fact that God did not design the woman to take on the *burden of responsibilities* for the entire family should be honored and appreciated! Peter said that they should be *honored*, not as a lesser vessel, but honored in the uniqueness of their design...

Other translations interpret the role of "Help meet" as "*a helper fit for him*" (RSV), "*a helper as his partner*" (NRS), "*a helper comparable to him*" (NKJ) or "*an helper as his counterpart*" (YLT).

These phrases indicate that the wife is to provide assistance wherever *"Help"* is needed! So although she is not directly and overall responsible for leading the family, she can still *help to lead* the family. And though she is not the primary provider, she can *help to contribute* if this is where the help is needed. Or while she may not be the "house-band", she can *lend support to,* and *help strengthen* or *reinforce* the stability of the house.

After God planted the Garden of Eden, the Bible said that He took the man and put him into the Garden to dress it and to keep it (*that was his job – he was directly responsible*). God gave him the command of *what was* and *was not* allowed (*Gen:2:16-17: again, making him directly responsible*).

Gen:2:18:

And the LORD God said, It is not good that the man should be alone; I will make him an help meet for him.

Verse:22

And the rib, which the LORD God had taken from man, made he a woman, and brought her unto the man. KJV

By the time God brought Adam his wife, He had already given him purpose, a vision, and a job – she was made for the purpose of *assisting him*; to be *a suitable companion* for him, and to *support him* and *the purpose* that God had given him. Some may say that this seems a bit one-sided; it seems to be all about the man. But actually, God gave a specific design to the family so that the entire family unit can be amazingly blessed, but everyone in the union must function as they were designed.

If a Single woman already has a purpose and a Vision for her life – and then she decides to get married, *Wisdom* would tell her to make sure that her *future husband* shares her Vision and outlook on life, or is at least willing to compromise.

Because once she makes *the decision* to marry (*keeping in mind that it's her choice*), God will expect her to submit to, and become "*one*" with the Vision and purpose of her husband.

Chapter 9

Understanding the One I Love

Many conflicts occur within marriage simply because the couple have not taken the time to get to know and understand each other. Sure, they may have acquired some general knowledge of their Spouse, but did they get to know their character and personality? More often than not, disagreements and offense come about when there is a lack of understanding as to "why" a person do what they do, or say some of the things that they say! Having the ability to understand your Spouse, and to conduct yourself accordingly could be the key to a peaceful home.

Prov:4:7

Wisdom is the principal thing; therefore get wisdom: and with all thy getting get understanding.

~and 1Pt:3:7 instructs the husbands to:

"...dwell with the wives according to knowledge."

These passages help us to see that it would do us well to have a working knowledge, or an understanding of our Spouse!

The first twelve years of our marriage was extremely turbulent, until my wife and I attended a Relationship Building Certification Course called the ARYA Project. It wasn't until then that we realized that our biggest issue had nothing to do with us loving each other, or being incompatible – it was the fact that we simply did not understand each other's character and personality! But once we gained an understanding, it brought us a tremendous amount of peace, and closer than ever before!

A person's internal make-up could possibly range from one extreme to another. Some people have a very pessimistic personality, and some are very optimistic.

Pessimism

A pessimistic person is a very negative person; a person who expects bad things to happen; they often have the attitude (1) "I'll believe it when I see it", (2) "Nothing good ever happens to me", or (3) If something good happens, it's a FLUKE!

Simpson, Kelly. ARYA Project.2004

Optimism

An optimistic person is (1) a very positive person, (2) one who always looks on the brighter side of things, or (3) a very hopeful person. Which is the way that every Bible believing Christian should be, or strive to be!

Simpson, Kelly. ARYA Project.2004

1Pt:1:3 says,

> "...according to His abundant mercy, God had begotten us again unto a lively hope (or a living hope) by the resurrection of Jesus Christ from the dead. KJV

And 2Cor:5:7 says,

> "...we walk by faith, not by sight. KJV

So, if we are indeed people of faith, we should be very optimistic about every situation we encounter, because God has Anointed us to be victorious in Christ (Rom:8:37)!

If we happen to be the optimist in the relationship, and our spouse is the pessimist, it's not a good idea for us to put them down, but rather, to understand that they simply need time to grow in their faith.

Oftentimes, negative feelings are due to bad experiences, or constant let-downs in the past. They are usually associated with *"wounds"* in the emotions and can only be healed by learning to put faith in God's promises (i.e. His Word).

Rom:10:17:

...faith cometh by hearing, and hearing by the word of God. KJV

The more they hear the Word of God, the more their faith will grow, and the more healing will manifest, eventually causing the negativity to dissipate from their heart. As a loving spouse, your patience and understanding, along with positive reinforcements of encouragement will aid in their healing process.

Another personality conflict that occurs between couples is where one may be an "Introvert", and the other one is an "Extrovert".

Introverts

Introverts are often quiet and are referred to as listeners. They feel very deep emotions just like anyone else, but many times they choose not to share what they are feeling. When an introvert is quietly listening, it doesn't mean that they necessarily agree with "what's being said". Introverts like to be able to process information through their mind before they respond. And probably most importantly, introverts enjoy their "alone-time". It has absolutely nothing to do with you (the Spouse) – it's just a part of their make-up; it's the way they're wired; it's just "who" they are!

Simpson, Kelly. ARYA Project.2004

Extroverts

In direct contrast, the "Extrovert" is a very outward, or outgoing person! They are often said to be out-spoken or talkative. They "love" and "live" to be around people! More often than not, extroverts can be very good at talking, but may not be very good listeners. Extroverts seem to formulate plans or ideas out-loud as thoughts come to their minds and deal with the consequences later, should they arise. Extroverts seem to enjoy the company of introverts, because they listen more than they talk! Nevertheless, it's very possible for an extrovert to have "introvert characteristics", and vice-versa.

Simpson, Kelly. ARYA Project.2004

Couples who understand their spouse's personality seem to have less disagreement and are able to cohabitate better, because they are not constantly guessing why the other one responds or behaves the way they do, alleviating the opportunity for offence.

Assuming Good-will

Assuming good-will is the method by which one gives their Spouse the benefit of the doubt by assuming the best about a given situation, and not the worst.

Simpson, Kelly. ARYA Project.2004

Instead of immediately jumping to conclusions and assuming the worst, attempt to view your Spouse, their motives or intentions in a positive light. Assume that they may have meant to say things another way; assume that they may have had a bad day; assume that they did not see your missed call, and etc. DO NOT TRY reading their thoughts or facial expressions, ASSUME the BEST of them! After all, if there's anyone on planet earth that you ought to be able to give *the benefit of the doubt to*, it ought to be your Spouse; it ought to be the one YOU CHOSE to marry!

If a Spouse is pessimistic, or if they have had a number of negative experiences where their trust has been broken over and over again, this method will require a *"major mind-set overhaul"* in order to accomplish this. Which means that forgiveness will certainly be in order, and you'll have to learn to trust all over again! Although, those negative feelings and emotions may still be there for a while, just keep reminding yourself that this is *to better your relationship,* and to *give you peace of mind.* No doubt, it's going to take practice, practice, practice! But you can do it! Especially if you know in your heart that you're going to "stay" in the relationship! As frustrating, and as turbulent as it may get at times, if you know that you're going to stay, "don't live in misery!" Make the BEST of your relationship and give yourself the gift of peace!

Chapter 10

The Bedroom of the Believer

What goes on *in the bedroom* of *married Believers* has been a mysterious and controversial topic in the body of Christ for decades. We've been approached for years with questions that center around, "What is right in the eyes of God; what's legal in the bedroom of God-fearing marriages; what does God approve of sexually?"

We've heard many responses and opinions to questions like this, but we didn't want to give our own personal opinion; nor did we want to merely repeat what someone else had said. But we wanted to give a clear and concise answer from the Word of God so that couples could be free to enjoy their gift of marriage!

Now, I'm fully aware that some may not agree with my view, and that's ok! But I can say this, that my view is based on the Word of God, and I've not seen any other evidence that proves me otherwise in the Scripture!

The Bible teaches that marriage is *"honorable"* in every way, and the bedroom cannot be defiled or perverted (*Heb:13:4*). Honor carries the definition of *deserving the upmost respect*. It means that it has *an untarnished reputation*, and is likely *untarnishable*. It has the virtues of *truthfulness, candor* and stresses the *consciousness of choice*. So let's closely examine the Scripture:

Heb:13:4

Marriage is honourable in all, and the bed undefiled: but whoremongers and adulterers God will judge. KJV

The Scripture is clearly stating that, "*God honors the bedroom of the married,*" and there is no indication that there is "*judgment*" towards their bedroom. However, there are emphasis of judgment being placed where there is *sexual immorality*! The writer says, that it's *"the whoremongers and adulterers that God will judge."* Well, the *"married"* does not fall up under this class of people. This tells me that God has such a high regard for marriage, that *"not even He"* passes judgment on their bedroom! But He does take major issue where there is *sexual immorality*. In fact, every place throughout Scripture where God takes an issue with sex, is when there was perversion outside the confines of marriage. But never do you find God bringing judgment where there is a Covenant of marriage!

So, does that mean that multiple position and styles of sex are ok within marriage? It appears to be so according to God's Word, because He does not judge the bedroom that fall into the parameters of marriage. In my own personal opinion, the only way that I can see God getting involved is, if a violation of some sort occurs: i.e. to participate in an act that convicts you of your faith. Otherwise, if there is agreement between the two of you, and you both have a clear conscience, then God doesn't get involved!

I would stress however, that there should be absolute agreement in whatever you do, and you must do it by faith! Meaning your conscience must allow you to be able to do it "free of guilt", otherwise, you'll be in jeopardy of entering into sin!

> *Rom:14:22*
>
> *Hast thou faith? have it to thyself before God. Happy is he that condemneth not himself in that thing which he alloweth.*
>
> *Verse 23b says: "...for whatsoever is not of faith is sin."*

Like so many gifts that God has given to us, the Enemy (Satan) has taken and perverted it to the point that the ones to whom it was intended for cannot fully enjoy and appreciate the liberties God has given them. God provided a safe place for a man and woman to express and enjoy one another sexually free from judgment, and that's in the confines of marriage. Paul says, "to avoid sexual immorality, let every man have his own wife, and let every woman have her own husband… (*1Cor:7:1*-2)" This is that safe place!

When a couple "marries", their body no longer belongs to them, but it's "*a gift*" to their spouse! If you marry, and your spouse does not have full access to you when they need you – you are in *direct violation* of the Scripture, and your marriage is NOT by God's design!

> 1Cor:7:4:
>
> *The wife hath not power of her own body, but the husband: and likewise also the husband hath not power of his own body, but the wife.*

That means that the aged-old excuse of, "*Not tonight, I have a headache,*" is a violation of God's Word. It means that if your spouse needs you sexually, they have *a Biblical right* to your body. Now of course, as a loving and caring spouse, they may understand, honor and respect your situation or request – but Biblically, they reserve the right to respond as they have need without violating God's Word.

The only time the Bible gives a suggestion of withholding one's self, or reframing from sex is during a time of fasting and prayer – but even with that, it must be with the consent of your spouse.

1Cor:7:5:

Defraud ye not one the other, except it be with consent for a time, that ye may give yourselves to fasting and prayer; and come together again, that Satan tempt you not for your incontinency.

If your Spouse needs you, this doesn't mean that you cannot fast! It just means that you will not be able to offer *that part* of your body in the fast in worship to God – but Scripturally, God will understand…

Because of a lack of understanding of the Scriptures, many Christ-centered marriages are failing because they are not ministering to the sexual needs of their spouse – after God has made the provisions for it. Many are fantasying about the world's sexual liberties, not realizing that *"those liberties"* were not intended for the world, but they were meant for Covenants who honor God thru marriage.

If this Biblical view is too much for you to bear, I would advise you "Not to practice it," because your lack of faith has condemned you already! But for those who could receive it – "Enjoy your spouse – your gift from God!"

Chapter 11

Is Divorce a Biblical Option?

Another frequently debated topic in the body of Christ is one that centers around the discussion of "divorce". Again, there are many different views and opinions, but the Word of God reveals God's position on the issue, and how He does not waiver!

Marriage by God's design is a lifetime commitment! According to Scripture, the "Law of marriage" is unto death.

1Cor:7:39:

The wife is bound by the law as long as her husband liveth; but if her husband be dead, she is at liberty to be married to whom she will; only in the Lord.

Rom:7:2-3

For the woman which hath an husband is bound by the law to her husband so long as he liveth; but if the husband be dead, she is loosed from the law of her husband. So then if, while her husband liveth, she be married to another man, she shall be called an adulteress: but if her husband be dead, she is free from that law; so that she is no adulteress, though she be married to another man.

The "Law of marriage" reveals that "in God's eyes," the ONLY thing that can legally disannul the Covenant between husband and wife is death, or a case where infidelity is involved.

Mt:19:3

The Pharisees also came unto him, tempting him, and saying unto him, Is it lawful for a man to put away his wife for every cause?

Verse:4-6

And he answered and said unto them, **Have ye not read**, *that he which made them* **at the beginning** *made them* **male** *and* **female**, *And said,* **For this cause** *shall a man* **leave** *father and mother, and shall* **cleave** *to his wife: and they twain shall be* **one flesh**? *Wherefore they are* **no more twain**, *but* **one flesh**. *What therefore* **God hath joined** *together, let not man put asunder.*

Verse:7-

They say unto him, Why did Moses then command to give a writing of divorcement, and to put her away? He saith unto them, Moses because of the **hardness of your hearts** *suffered you to put away your wives:* **but from the beginning it was not so.** *And I say unto you, Whosoever shall put away his wife,* **except it be for fornication**, *and shall marry another,* **committeth**

> ***adultery**: and whoso marrieth her which is put away doth commit adultery.*

When the issue of divorce was presented to Jesus, the first thing He did was take them back to *God's original design* for marriage. Denoting, when a man takes to himself a wife, God expects for him to leave and cleave! He is to leave father and mother, and in marriage – form one union with his wife, without any intentions of ever severing the union. This is why He said, *"What therefore God hath joined together, let not man put asunder"* (Mt:19:6).

Jesus goes on to acknowledge that yes, Moses made provisions under the law for divorce, but then announced that it was never part of *God's original design* for marriage – in other words, it was never His Will (Mt:19:8). Jesus explained that Moses only wrote the command because of the hardness of their hearts. And sadly, that is why so many divorces occur, even throughout the body of Christ – it's because of the *hardness of hearts,* or *selfishness.*

The Most Common Reasons for Divorce

When couples give room to pride; carnal lust; broken-trust; grief or pain; the weariness of hardship or struggle, or the experience of a broken-heart – these are all contributors to the hardening of a heart. And eventually, the person will begin responding as an individual, and not as someone who's in Covenant – and their life will become solely about *"them and what they want"*, and may potentially desire a divorce.

Some of the most common reasons that marriages end in divorce are (1) poor communication, (2) financial challenges, (3) issues with commitment, (4) changes in priorities, (5) infidelity, (6) unmet needs and failed expectations, (7) addictions (i.e. drug, alcohol, porn, or etc.), (8) parenting differences, (9) "quote/unquote" irreconcilable differences, (10) stepfamily issues, and (11) a lack of intimacy and love in the relationship.

But through humility and prayer, every one of these issues can be worked through, but it's going to require focus and a willing heart. And there are times when intervention may be necessary, especially when no one can get a word in edgewise. It would be wise to seek-out counsel from your Pastor or Spiritual Leader, and in some cases, it may be necessary to seek out professional counselors. But whatever the lack, difficulty, or the situation may be, God expects us to work through it, and/or work it out because of the choice and commitment we made before Him.

The Pharisees' question to Jesus revealed the selfishness of their hearts, and their irreverent approach to marriage! They asked Him, *"Is it lawful for a man to put away his wife for every cause?"* The phrase *"every cause"* shows the true intent of their hearts: the lack of love; the lack of commitment; the lack of unity. It reveals that their marriages were just about them! Apparently, they felt that if they couldn't have their way, then they should be able to divorce for any and every cause. But Jesus tells them in Mt:19:9, that **the only cause** they could *rightfully* put away their wives for was for **the cause** of **fornication**. Fornication is a Covenant breaker!

Biblically, besides the death of a spouse, fornication is the only other thing that voids the contract of marriage. Just as spiritual adultery or fornication breaks your Covenant with God (i.e. serving other gods, not putting Him first, disobeying His Will for your life, Deut:31:16-18; 1Chr:5:25-26; Ez:6:8-10; Ez:23:28-30), in the same way, fornication breaks the Covenant of marriage!

Separation

Although God does not condone, nor endorse divorce, there may be a case that warrants "a *period of separation,*" for which God has made provisions. This however, should *not* be *the first option*, but be *a last resort*. The only time that this may be a good idea is when the couple is not getting alone at all; they're constantly at odds on a daily basis; emotions and tensions between the two are steadily rising, and thoughts of hurting yourself or the other person is a constant temptation! The best idea may be to *remove yourself* from the hostile environment to give the both of you time and space to cool-down, and consider the things that are most important, such as: how far you've come together in life; the love, sweat and tears you've invested in each other; the victories you've already won together, and/or the welfare of your children (if applicable). Take 'that time' to really weigh the *importance of the issues* or *disagreements* that are currently at hand.

Paul says this concerning separation:

1Cor:7:10-11

*And unto the married I command, yet not I, but the Lord, Let not the wife depart from her husband: But and **if she depart**, let her remain unmarried, **or be reconciled** to **her husband**: and let not the husband put away his wife.*

If she departs the home of her husband for a period of time, and returns to be reconciled to him, this would be a *"period of separation"*. While it *may not be idea* for some, it may very-well be *necessary*. But it should be done with *the objective* to process through that temporary, but difficult time, while focusing on the possibilities of *reconciliation*.

The Importance of Premarital Counseling

Marriage is a Covenant that should never be entered into lightly. A great deal of thought and consideration should be given to this life-long commitment! Which is why premarital counseling is *so vitally important*. It helps you to see and consider some things that you *may not* have given serious thought to. If you enter the marriage haphazardly, having little knowledge of the commitment you're about to make, or having minimum knowledge of the person you're going to marry: i.e. their lifestyle, their habits, their financial condition and obligations, their family status (i.e. children from previous relationships); their dreams, goals and vision for life and family, well God still expects you to honor the Covenant until "death separates you".

The Bibles says that after Jesus finished speaking with the Pharisees, the disciples asked Him about marriage again once they went in the house (*Mk:10:10*), and Jesus explained a second time. Then the disciples said in Mt:19:10, "*If this be the case (concerning marriage)* (paraphrasing), *it is not good to marry.*" And immediately following, Jesus told them (*in a nutshell*) that marriage isn't for everyone (*Mt:19:11-12*)!

Abuse in Marriage

Sexual, physical and/or verbal abuse is never acceptable in the Covenant of marriage. Such behavior is *demonic in nature* and *violates* the very purpose of the union. Paul said,

"For no man ever yet hated his own flesh; but nourisheth and cherisheth it, even as the Lord the church" (Eph:5:29). When a marital relationship reaches a point where it's *toxic* and is *no longer healthy*, wisdom would say *seek godly counsel* coupled *with prayer*, and allow God to lead you in your next move. Even if it means, being by yourself: *"But and if she depart, let her remain unmarried…"* (1Cor:7:11).

Is Divorce Forgivable?

Many want to know, *"Is divorce forgivable? If a person repents – will God forgive divorce for reasons other than fornication?"* The Bible is clear that God forgives *all sin*, with the exception of blasphemy against the Holy Ghost (Mt:12:31-32). However, that does not mean that God changed His stance or position on marriage being a lifetime commitment! *Nor does it* give a person permission to divorce for any other reason other than fornication. But *it does mean* that *God is merciful* and *will forgive* your sin. In my view, *divorce* is as much *of a choice* as *getting married*! But as a believer, these decisions must be done with *reverential fear* and *God-consciousness* towards God.

Phil:2:12b

…work out your own salvation with fear and trembling.

In addition, those decisions must be decided by faith. Only faith will allow you to move past your mistakes, and have a clear conscience towards God.

Rom:14:22-23

Hast thou faith? have it to thyself before God. Happy is he that condemneth not himself in that thing which he alloweth. And he that doubteth is damned if he eat, because he eateth not of faith: for whatsoever is not of faith is sin.

Chapter 12

A Guide to Premarital Counseling

As a Pastor, I feel that the office we hold obligates us to help those who are considering marriage in making good sound decisions for their lives. This is where Premarital Counseling proves to be a valuable tool!

The counseling sessions should be done in preferably a private, non-threating, non-intimidating environment, where the couple could feel free to open-up and express intimate details concerning their relationship. Our job is merely to facilitate and guide the discussion, helping them to identify and consider some potential challenges, pitfalls and areas in the relationship that may need some attention.

These counseling sessions are not by any means a "fix-all," nor are the *suggested topics* enclosed *"all conclusive."* Nonetheless, the objective is to set the couple on a path that could lead them to success!

Suggested Topics for Discussion

Evidence of effective counseling sessions are the fact that you will not be able to complete *the suggested topics* in only one setting. Because the couples will become so involved in exploring their relationship, that you will have to break the discussions up into multiple sessions. And since some topics will no doubt be more in-depth than others, some sessions will take a lot longer to discuss!

It's extremely valuable to get the couple to open-up and lay-out all of the important and concealed issues on the table. Getting them to think about *"how they feel"* about them, and *"how they plan"* to handle them will be of great service to them in the long run! Even if they begin arguing during the session, or call the wedding off, then the premarital counseling would have been a tremendous success!

1. Why Marry?
    - Lead the couples in a discussion on "why" do they feel that they want to get married?
    - One at a time, have them to express their thoughts to each other, "Why they love each other?" Have them to speak on the things that they value and appreciate about their mate

2. Have an open discussion about the most common reasons that marriages fail (discussed in Chapter 11): (i.e. poor communication; financial problems; commitment problems; changes in priorities; infidelity issues; unmet needs and failed expectations; addictions (drug, alcohol, porn, or etc.); parenting differences and stepfamily issues; irreconcilable

differences; a lack of intimacy and love in the relationship)

- ➤ Try to identify if any of these issues currently exist in their relationship
- ➤ If so, how they are handling them? Or how do they plan to handle them?

3. Help them to understand that marriage is their choice! That they are making a conscience decision to enter into Covenant with this person – with all of their flaws, short-comings; faults, indiscretions, failures, weaknesses and etc. (discussed in Chapter 6)
    - ➤ That they are consciously entering into a "lifetime commitment," and God expects them to honor it

4. Allow (one at a time) to discuss their view and vision for marriage, family and life – and how do they plan to unite their vision (see Chapter 7)
    - ➤ Discuss goals: short-term and long-term

- ➤ The objective is to get them thinking about and discussing their future as they see it, and to talk about their willingness to compromise if they see things differently

5. Give a clear understanding to what is meant by becoming one flesh; explain the process (see Chapters 5 & 6)

6. Explain the roles and responsibilities of a godly marriage (see Chapter 8)
    - ➤ Help them to understand God's framework for marriage as outlined in Ephesians Chapter Five
    - ➤ Discuss the Biblical roles and responsibilities of both the husband and the wife
    - ➤ Help them to realize the weight of each role
    - ➤ Get them to see that they are volunteering to take on these challenging responsibilities!

7. Ask questions that possibly had not been asked or considered:
    - Have you ever been married before?
    - Are you married now?
    - Are there any ties or connections to any other family or individuals that your fiancé does not know about? (i.e. a family in another city, state or country; a husband or a wife you're legally bound to; have you any children given in adoption, and etc.)

8. Discuss the issue of kids:
    - Do you want children (or want any more)?
    - Are you in agreement on discipline and privileges?
    - If it's a blended family: What rights or permissions do the other parent have? Does the biological parent agree whole-heartedly with those permissions?

- How will you handle "baby-daddy" or "baby-momma" *drama* (*or* issues)? What's the approach to addressing them?

9. Discuss: How will the finances be managed:
   - Will there be combined or separate Bank accounts, or both?
   - If combined accounts, who will manage them? It's always best to play to your strengths – it's wise to allow the one who has the most financial discipline to manage the income

There are many opinions about how combining finances *pertains to oneness*. But "oneness" is revealed through "the ability to agree or be together in agreement!" What may work well for one couple, may not work well for another. There may be issues of excessive spending; prioritizing; selfishness. Or a couple may simply be divided in their views on how the monies should be managed. If "what they are doing" is causing confusion, or arguments, or major disagreements – then *that's not oneness!* Wisdom would say, for the benefit of the marriage, find a method that works best for them and establish an agreement! If they are able to "walk together in agreement", then *that's oneness*!

- ➢ Does the couple have a budget? If not, offer to help them to devise one
- ➢ Are there any outstanding debts or loans that the other one doesn't know about?
- ➢ Do they have or plan to get medical or life insurance?

10. Discuss the topic: Understanding the one I love (see Chapter 9)
- ➢ Identifying your mate's personality: Optimism or pessimism; Introvert or Extrovert
- ➢ Discuss: Learning to assume "good will"
- ➢ Discuss: Keeping the "Honey" in the "Moon" (honeymoon) – "What it takes to catch them, will require that and more to keep them!" The Point: Don't become complacent or stagnated in your ministry to your spouse

11. The Bedroom of the Believer (see Chapter 10)
    - ➤ Help the couple to understand their liberty in the bedroom; that God does not judge the bedroom of the married, and neither should anyone else (*Heb:13:4*)
    - ➤ There is no condemnation for what is done between the couple in the privacy of their bedroom, as long as it doesn't convict their conscience (*Rom:14:23b*)
    - ➤ The bedroom of the married need not fear the judgement of God, He has reserved His judgment for the sexually immoral (*Heb:13:4*)

www.ingramcontent.com/pod-product-compliance
Lightning Source LLC
Chambersburg PA
CBHW050646160426
43194CB00010B/1824